READ

Man in the Moon

by Lada Josefa Kratky

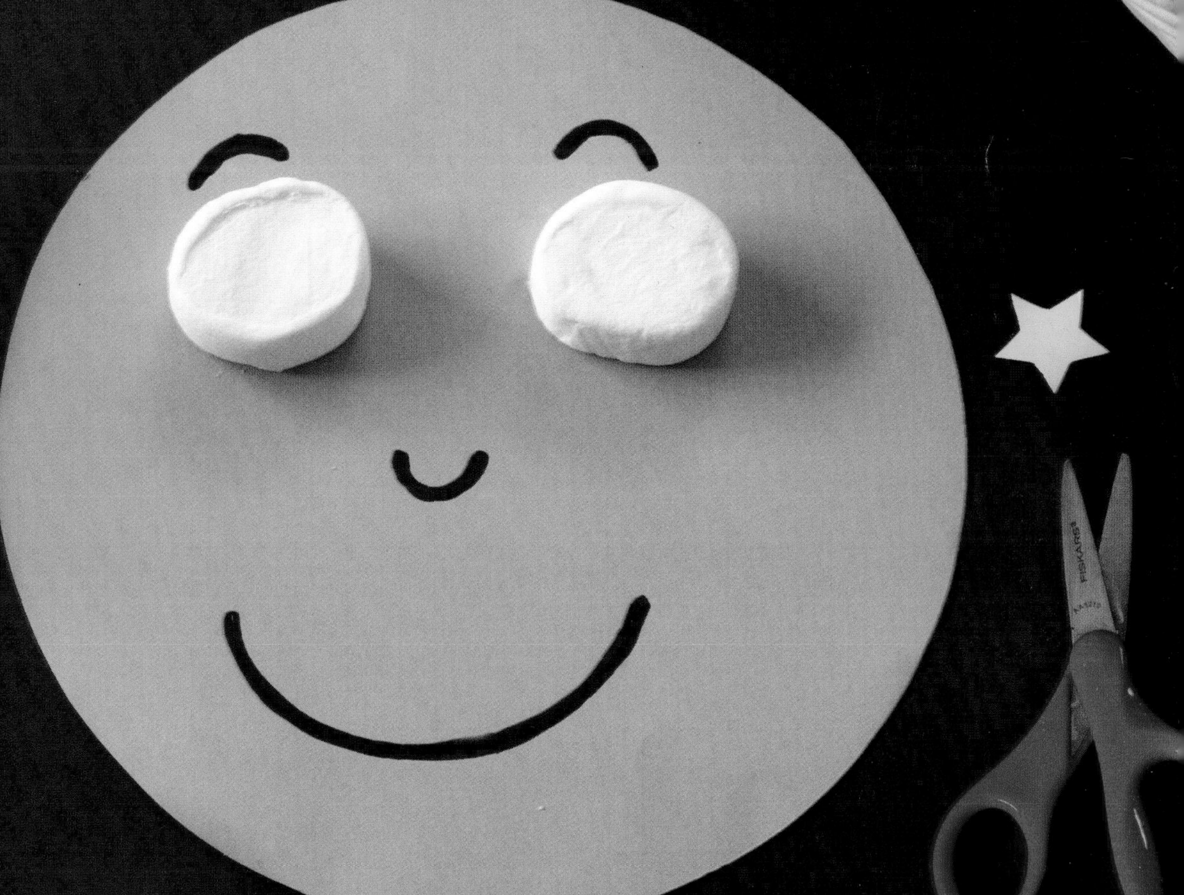

NATIONAL GEOGRAPHIC
School Publishing

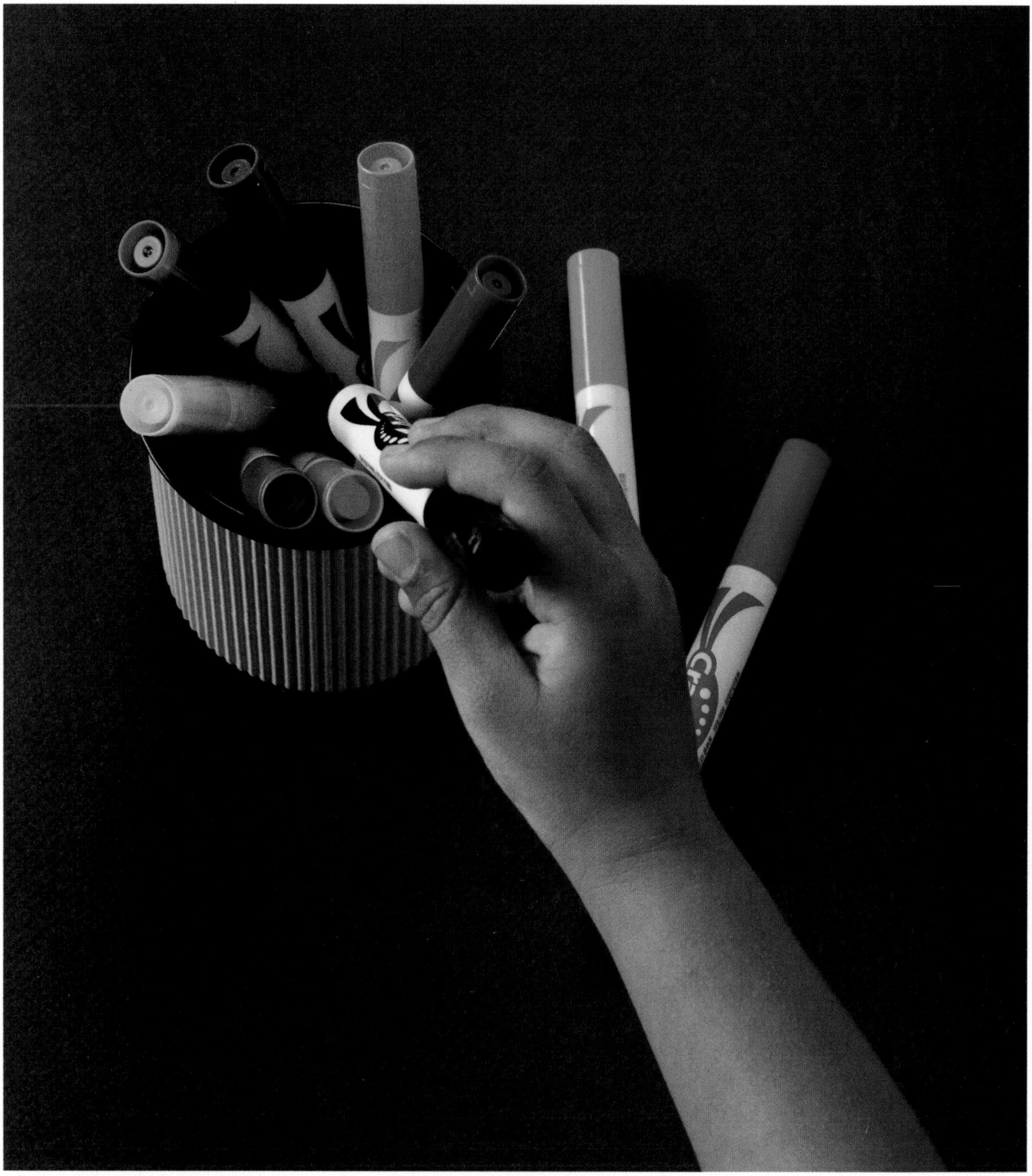

a 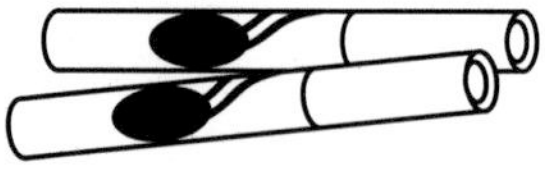

marker

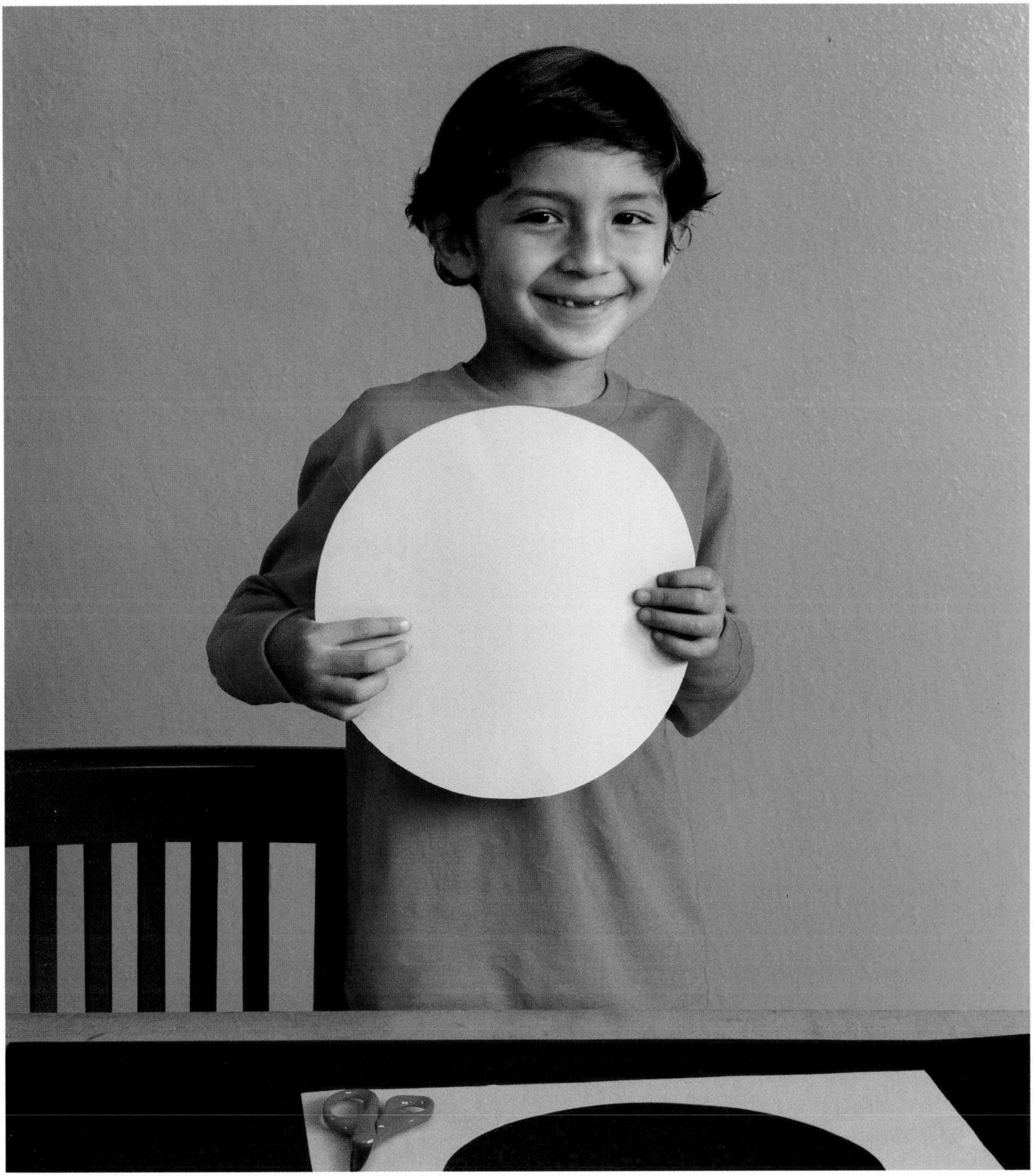

a 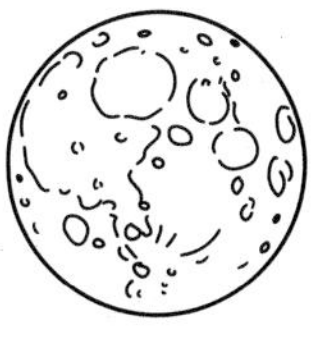

moon

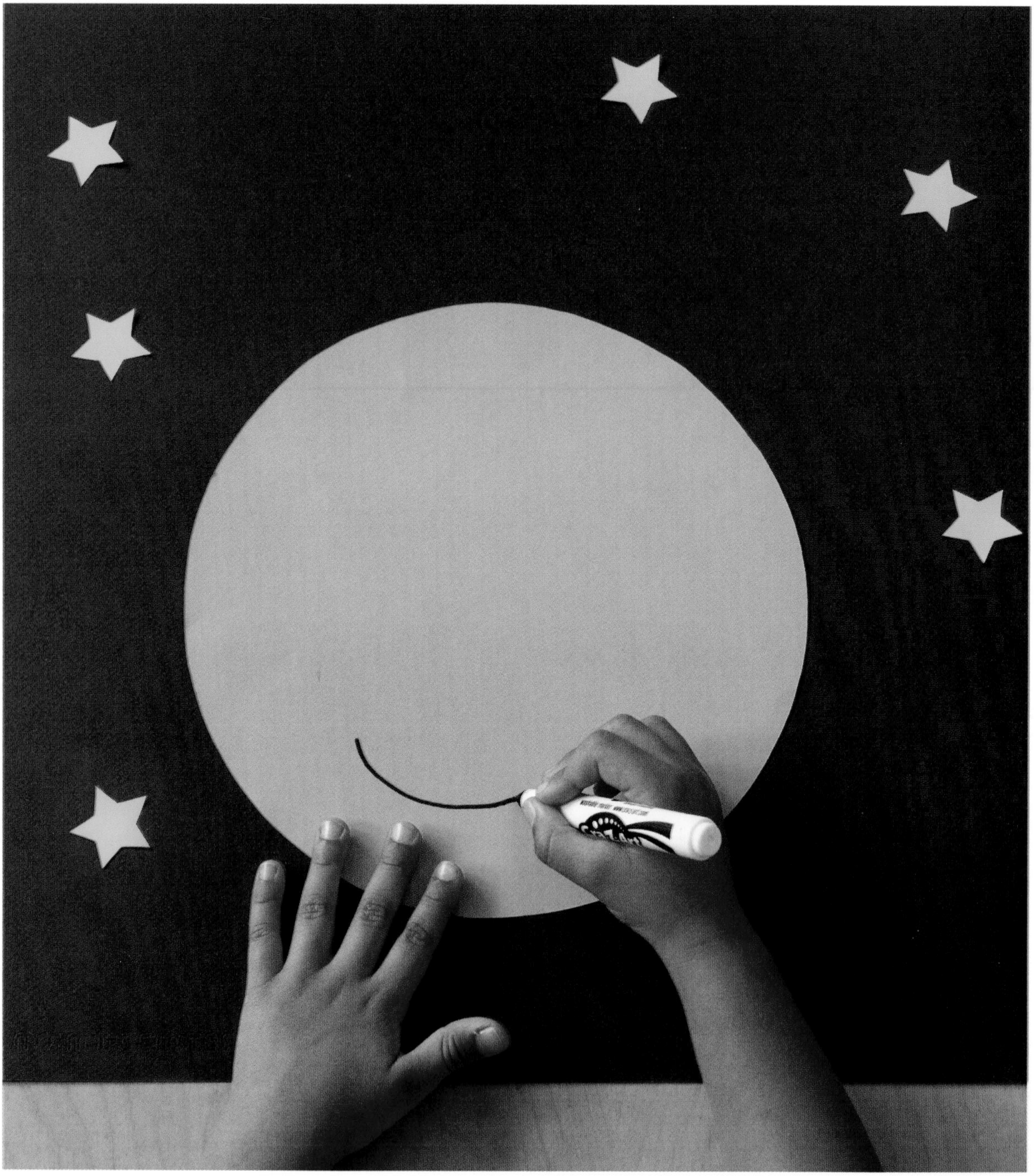

a 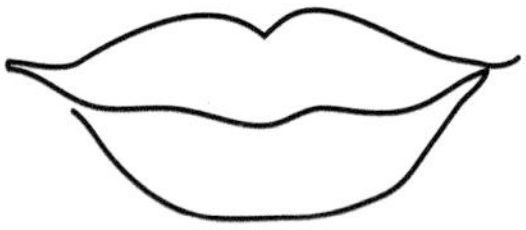

mouth

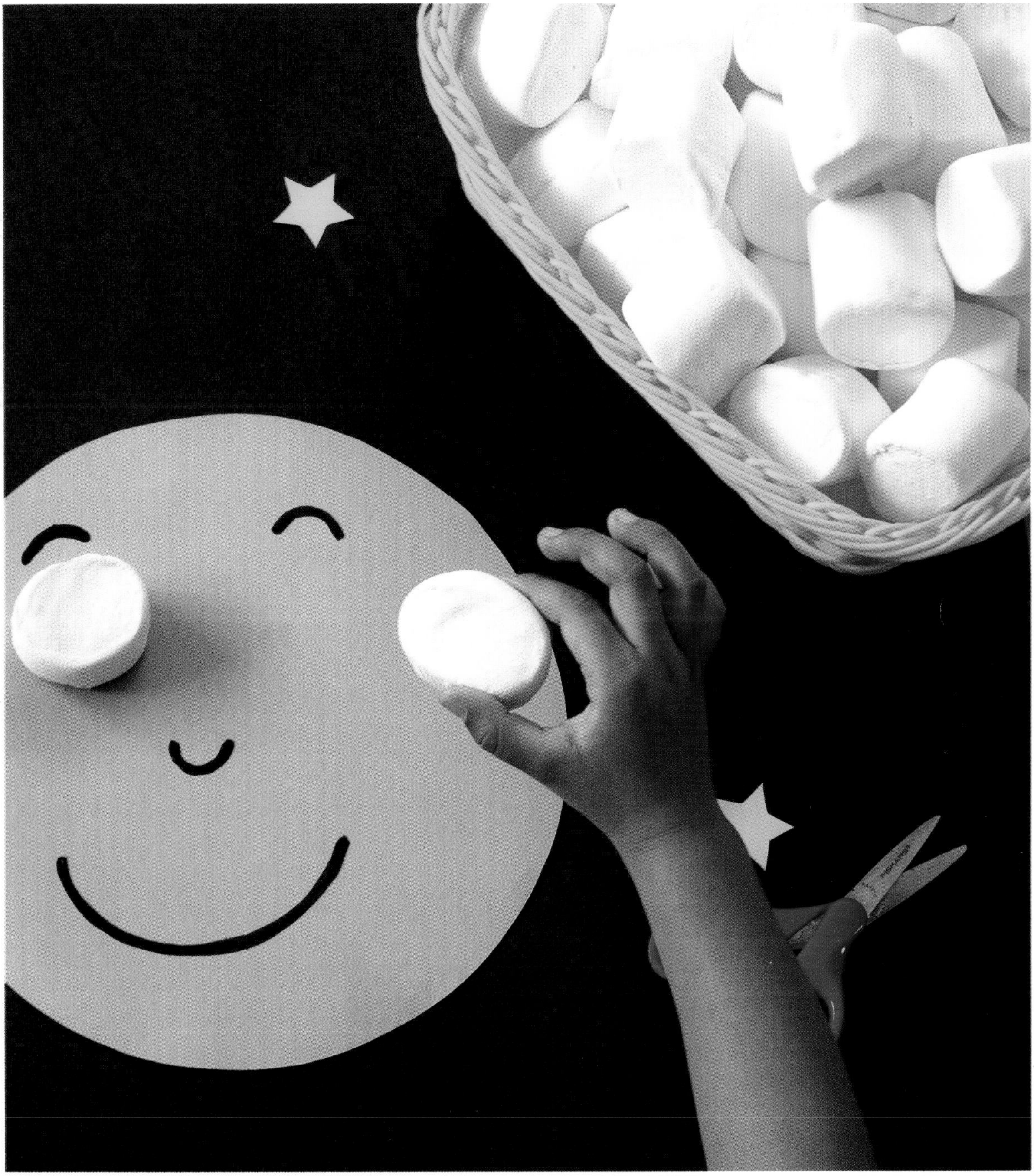

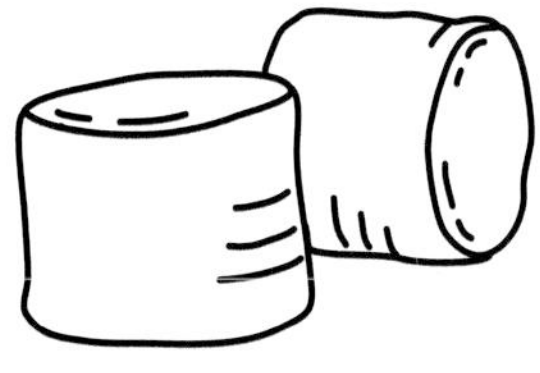

marshmallows

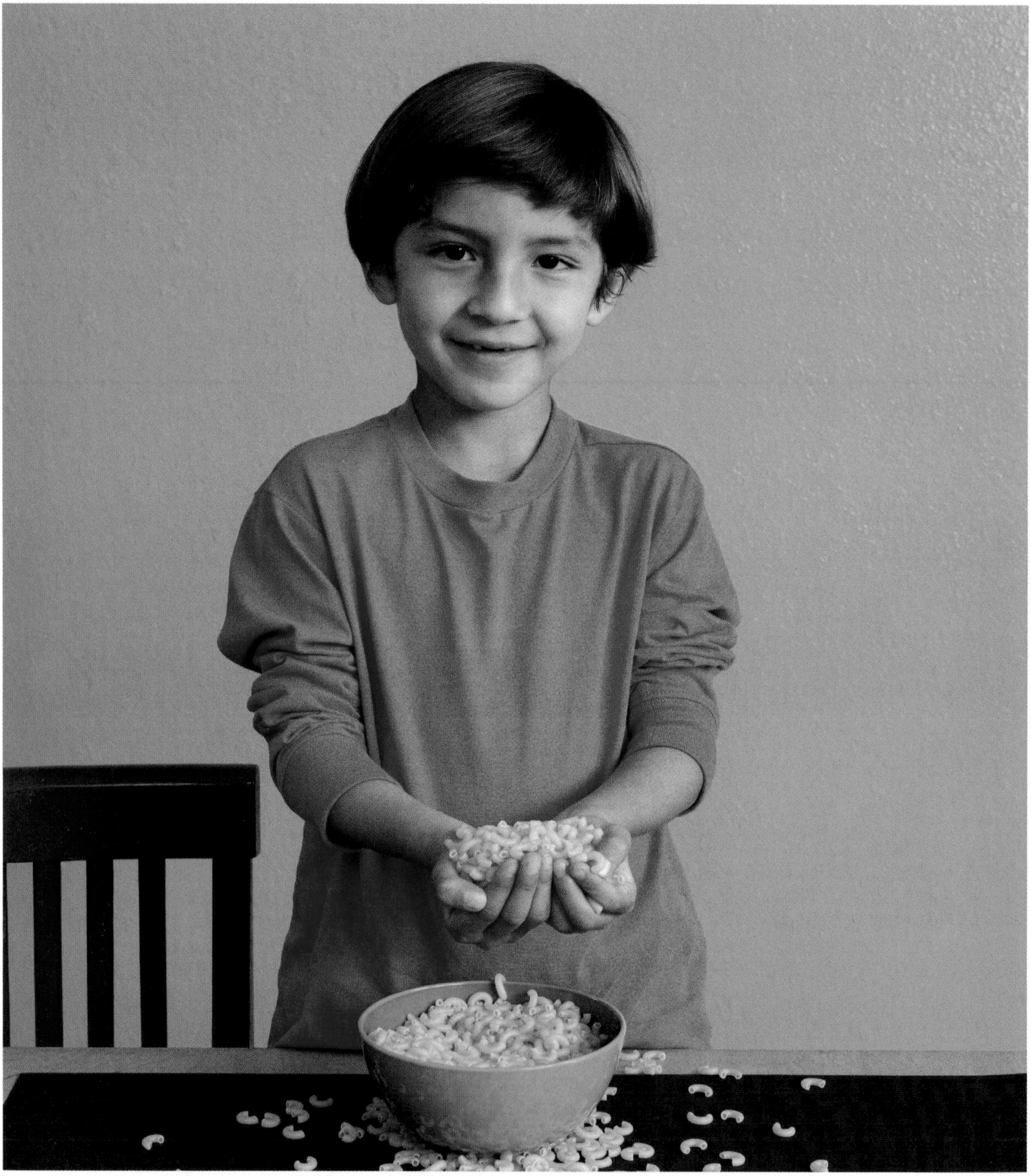

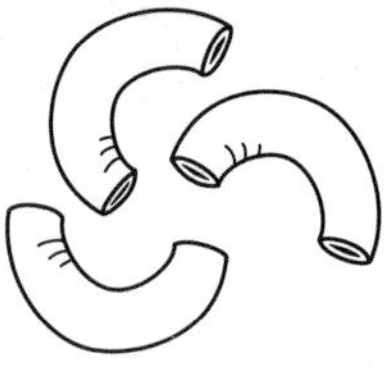

macaroni

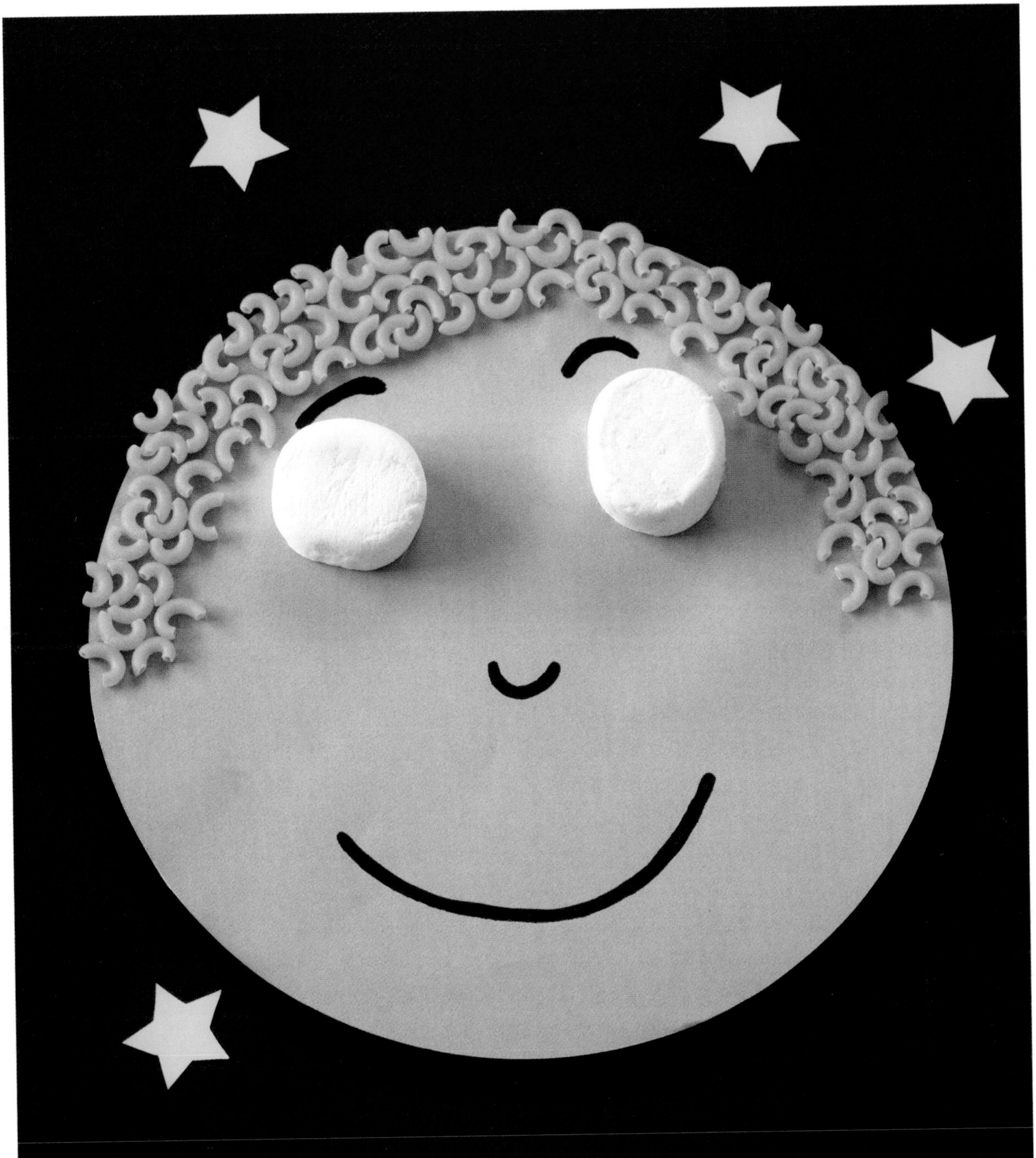

a 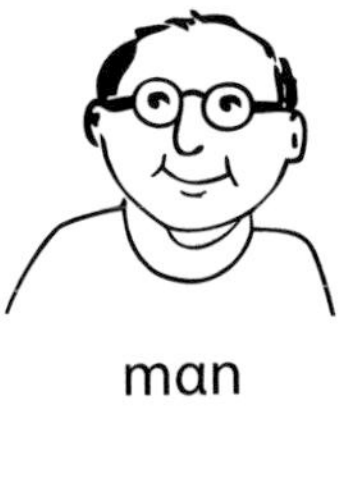

man

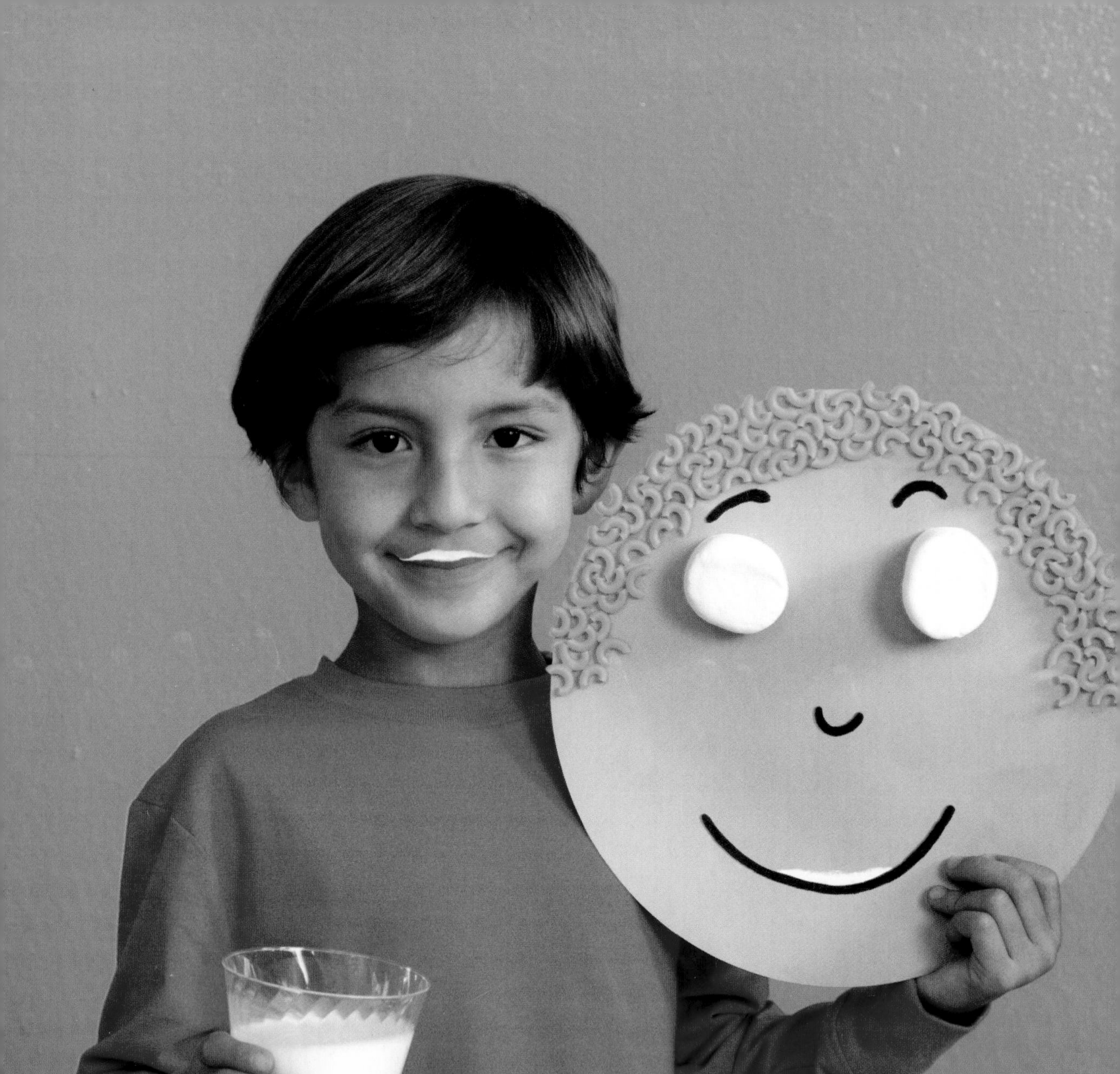

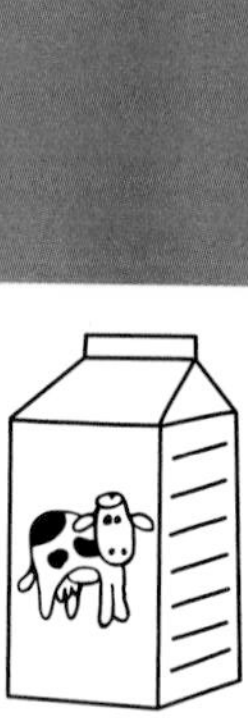

milk